GW01417688

A R R I V A L   P R E S S

FUNNY BONES

Edited by

TIM SHARP

First published in Great Britain in 1997 by
ARRIVAL PRESS
1-2 Wainman Road, Woodston,
Peterborough, PE2 7BU
Telephone (01733) 230762

HB ISBN 1 85786 666 5
SB ISBN 1 85786 671 1

FOREWORD

Funny Bones is an enlightening collection of verse by everyday people about things that amuse them. Whether it be a ditty about toilet paper or a visit to the dentists, all are covered within these pages.

Poetry is one of the best forms of relaxation and the poets in this anthology have expressed clearly their own special feelings to lighten the readers day.

This anthology is a must for everyone who loves to smile, and will keep you smiling for months to come. So relax and be reminded of the amusing days of our lives.

Tim Sharp
Editor

CONTENTS

A Horse In Lemon Time

There is no animal quite like
a horse in Lemon Time,
as tossing wild his tangled mane
he gallops forth across the plain
seeking that place among the groves
where bitter-sweet xanthippe roves.
There is no animal quite like
a horse in Lemon Time

- Unless it be the saw-toothed sloth
that dwells in ancient towers
and drops with sudden red-eyed wrath
upon the Turk and Visigoth
to cling to their mustachios
and nibble their pistachios.
There is no animal quite like that!
- Unless it is our cat

There in a cosy corner curled
she lazes all serene
who knows what goes on in her head!
She rises only to be fed
or sneer at every human slave,
the way all good cats should behave.
No creature is there in the world
quite like the feline queen!

W Blacklaw

TRIP TO REMEMBER

Whilst shopping with my husband
Too the warehouse we went
He runs a small garage shop
And is trying to extend.
Bottles of drinks crisps and sweets
We brought them by the score
Was this an exciting venture
No it was such a very big bore
Then I noticed something out of my eye
And thought I must have that
It would go with the colour in my kitchen
And sit where the microwave sat.
My husband brought himself a bin
To stay in his office by the door
It was my suggestion cause he throws paper on the floor
We finished the shopping after some time
To the car park we did go
But we could not see the car anywhere
So a hunting we went to and fro
After about quarter of an hour we spotted our old car
It seems I had walked for hours but it wasn't really far
Unloading the shopping, my husband packing the unbreakables first
He said 'Stretch out your arms and hold all this'
I had worked up quite a thirst
At last the red bin he'd brought but he didn't know what to do
So he stuck it over my head so tight
I didn't have a clue
He walked off to take the trolley back
And left me standing there
Shouting out 'This isn't funny anymore' as if he didn't care
Ten minutes later he returned and, took the bin off again
People around were laughing at me
As if I were insane.

I don't go there anymore because I felt quite silly
Looking back I can see the funny side
  And our friends all laugh until they're dizzy

Jan Nice

A BLOW-WAVE

A young man who worked in the docks,
Was very proud of his curly locks
One day to his dismay
His toupee blew away
Out to sea, where it grounded on the rocks.

Barbara Sowden

UNTITLED

The Incredible Hulk wasn't keen
On the recent change in attitudes he'd seen!
'For,' he said with a sulk,
'I'll have only my bulk,
If the *whole world* intends *going green*!'

Pauline Thomas

JOB INTERVIEW

Pay to be discussed. (Disgust!)
Hours (ours) to be arranged.
I think I'm gettin' the job interview now.
Don't call me. I'll call you.

Angie Garrett

GIVING 'EM THE BIRD

Doreen the pensioner
  lived in a flat,
she grumbled it was too high
she wanted something lower
not a home up in the sky.

So to the city council
  she did go
stating she wanted a bungalow
she complained to the council, 'This is absurd
it's alright high up if you're crossed with a bird.'

Yvonne Bacon

COMMUNICATION DIFFICULTIES

There was a young fellow named Ray
I wrote him a letter one day
It was so absurd
Not a word had he heard,
But he said that he saw what I say.

Peter Sutton

TRAINING FOR THE CATWALK

Coastal walking is my leisure,
Giving me endless hours of pleasure.
Winter gear had room for change
So summer brought out top of the range.

Modelling never my career,
But maybe this is, getting nearer.
Though walking isn't really sports,
I felt competitive in these shorts.

Decisions, now, my manly chest,
Does it need a shirt or vest?
Boots a must, to create the walk
For heads to turn, and mouths to talk.

The hat, well, that did boost my ego,
It made me feel quite grand and regal.
Complete and ready, photo please!
Oh dear! I've overlooked my knees.

V Sharples

BEHIND THE BAR

Hello, I am Jayne, spelt with a 'Y'. And certainly not plain. Pulling pints in a pub now and again. It can be a very hard game. I see them come, see them go. 'Hello darling, alright?' 'See ya later, then!' 'Good night!'

After the consumers have drank a few pints of bitter. Some start to laugh and titter from the effects of the bitter. For them who drink lager, find bellies much larger. Oh what a sight.

When getting 'pissed', some dare to try a kiss. Some blokes go for a 'grope', but I still manage to cope.

After a few beers, some start acting the part very queer. Looking pale and white., with heads down bogs for the rest of the night.

There is some mind you, who are nice. Never looking twice.

Lady Jayne.

Oh no, not me. Well maybe, perhaps now and again.

Yes. I am Jayne in name, but certainly not plain. 'Last orders, time please!' 'Let's have those glasses!' 'Everybody out!' 'I'm glad that's over. Oh, what a night.

K M Jones

A YOUNG LADY FROM SCOLE

There was a young
Lady from Scole
While gardening fell
Down a hole
She went down a tunnel
Shaped like a funnel
And was invited to
Lunch by a mole

Iris Cracknell

ELECTION O'ER

Am gled it's oe'r
A could take nae mair
Election time am gled it's oe'r
Ma heid its ne'r been so sair
But the good thing noo
A hope heel be fair
Noo that Tony Blair's
In the chair
The opposition aw
Sittin' there looking glum
An sane it's not fair

J M Connelly

UNTITLED

When I was just a tiny tot,
I really was quite small,
On the table I liked to dance
Though my mother was scared I would fall.

Then one day as I danced around
I slipped and fell right off
'I bet your bottom's broken'
My mother, she did scoff.

With a tearful face, I managed a smile,
Though pleased I hadn't been smacked,
And said in all my innocence,
'Well, my bottom was already cracked!'

M I Robertson

SNAP HAPPY

'See Dad,
I was just sat sipping,
when I knew, that emu,
thought it was a coat at first
'till it nicked my drink,
then I thought,
hey, coats don't do that,
move around or even think.'
But I learned that day,
that I'll never play
or take a drink,
near the emu,
I once knew.

M Griffith

A Most Unusual Winter

The snow is thick and soft and white
Been coming down for half the night
And morning sheds an eerie light
On a most unusual winter.

Cars and lorries slide a bit
The council has no salt or grit
They said, 'We'd not expected it.'
What a most unusual winter.

Children shiver out of bed
And quickly build a make-shift sled
Then hurtle down to their elders' dread
In this most unusual winter.

The kettle fills the steaming cup
It's good to have a warming sup
But the heating bills go up and up
In this most unusual winter.

The car won't start, you need a hitch
You pile the clothes on, stitch by stitch
And the plumber's getting filthy rich
From this most unusual winter.

Each year we play this age-old game
Each winter different but the same
And we always, always put the blame
On a most unusual winter.

J Silver

SOAKED

I took a tea bag for a walk
We even had a little talk
Although quite vocal to the bag
Its silence came to be a drag
Not everyone would kindly bring
A tea bag on a piece of string
Letting it dangle by their side
While all around were mystified

Having spent some time together
Baggy was suffering from the weather
And so at last I set him free
To make his final cup of tea.

J Facchini

BETTER THAN THE GAP

A young girl, I'm told
has a tooth made out of gold
that is better than the gap she had before:
it gleams in the gloom
to illumine her dark bedroom
and can tune precisely into Radio Four!

Peter Comaish

BETHANY, AGED 1

Mummy thinks I'm messy,
But I don't think I am,
After all, this vanilla ice-cream
Could have been strawberry jam!

Yesterday it was custard
Now that was quite a treat,
But Mummy just couldn't understand
How I got it on my feet.

I think tomorrow's Friday
That could mean horrid fish
So when nobody's looking
I'll just throw it out of the dish!

Jennifer Rose

OWN GOAL

A footballer from Newcastle-upon-Tyne
Scored a goal for the very first time.
His team-mates were mad,
It was really quite sad.
He forgot they'd changed ends at half time!

Barbara Eyre

SOD THE WEATHER!

The other week the sun shone bright
It really was a lovely sight
But now it's dark and dull again
It really is a dreadful shame

The rain is pouring on the ground
I hate to hear the awful sound
Of cars a-splashing as they pass
I wish that Spring was here at last

My wellies I had put away
And my thick coat, so old and grey
But now I've got them out again
Oh what a bloody awful shame!

I'd like to make some salads fresh
And even wear a cheerful dress
But here I go still making stews
And plod along in thick, stout shoes

Oh damn the stupid awful weather
I think that we should wish together
For sunshine and for days so clear
Bad weather, you're not wanted here!

Jill Campbell

FACE CASE

I say, old chap, I know your face,
I've seen it at some other place.
But then perhaps I may be wrong,
Now, no offence, but had it long?

The other said with a trace of tears
I've had this face for years and years,
From east to west and north to south
I've had the same ears, nose and mouth.

The first man slowly scratched his head,
I'm absolutely sure, he said,
Lose confidence - retain no trace
Is one sure way to lose face.

The second said, I could agree
With what you say, but I foresee
That should I meet with some success
I'd just feel more confident I guess.

The first said, it's a bloody shame,
The second said, my mum's to blame,
And although I never knew my Dad
I reckon he was just as bad.

The first said, now don't despair,
After all you've got your hair
And although it looks grotesque,
It will serve you well in burlesque.

The second said, I no longer care,
When people passing stop and stare
You're lucky, man, you're not so cursed,
I couldn't face it, said the first.

Thomas Boyle

EARWIGGING

One day I said I'd love to be
A fly on someone's wall,
I'd eavesdrop every word they said,
I'd have myself a ball.

Soon after I'd expressed this wish,
I had a funny feeling,
And then I landed upside-down,
On Fred and Ethel's ceiling!

Now Fred and Ethel Blenkinsop,
We love them like no other,
For Eth's a sister to us all,
And Fred is like a brother.

It therefore came as quite a shock,
When Fred called me a creep,
And Ethel thought that you, my dear,
Were common, loud and cheap!

I crawled along the picture frame,
And almost fell, as Fred
Said every time I knocked his door,
It filled him full of dread!

They said our darling Rupert was
An utter little prig,
They said you lied about your age,
They knew I had a wig!

I settled on the mantelpiece,
And listened with alarm,
To folk I thought could never do
God's creatures any harm.

How wrong I was - for as I perched
A yard or so from Eth,
While slagging off my poetry
- She swatted me to death!

Peter Davies

MY NEW RIG-OUT

When I worked with Women's Aid, it really wasn't fair.
I never had the money to buy new clothes to wear.
And so when I told Sandra - life really was a drag,
Says she, 'Well Lil - find something in that heap of black bags.'

And what, you ask - did I find to wear?
Oh well now - let me see,
I found a floppy, purple hat,
With cherries, one, two, three.

A lovely green and yellow scarf
To hang around my neck
And the broadest pair of scuffed, brown boots
to hold me to the deck.

Then I found a mini-skirt
Blue, with big, white dots.
It was lying in the corner
hidden by some pots.

A pair of wynciette knickers
With elastic at the knees.
You need them because with mini-skirts
You're inclined to feel the breeze.
Then I found a lovely coat
With shoulder pads one foot wide
Quite handy 'cause when I see my tick-man
I can duck down my head and hide.

Aye! Those black bags came in real handy.
I'm dressed up like a toff!
The trouble is - you have no dress sense
That's why you sit and scoff!

Lily T Ross

ROAD TO HELL

My neighbour gave me two plants to pot
Keep them in your conservatory, where it is hot
She knew that my green fingers did not work very well
But this was a start that turned into the road to hell.

She called them 'Jade' plants which seemed a nice name
You can call them 'Money Plants' they are just the same
They will flower one day if they survive long enough
I must treat them kindly and not be too rough.

After one year, to propagate, some cuttings I did take
I potted them, as more money I wanted to make
They stand in lines on the conservatory floor
Already I have plants to the total of twenty four.

Each week I move and water them all outside
I stand and look at them with great pride
I march back with them through the doorway
But where is my money, they don't seem to pay.

I longed for the summer to put them in the sun
They do not like the elements, it is no fun
I have to nurture and give them tender care
They have me where they want me, leave them, I don't dare.

I wanted to give them names of their very own
They never complain or seem to moan
Not knowing the difference, it has to be said
I decided to give each one a number, instead.

I try talking to them, they never answer back
They are all well fed, for nothing they lack
When will I get a return from them all
It's like being in a lottery, their numbers never call
If my neighbour knew what she had started in the past
She would wonder how my collection has got so vast.

Alan Thorley

THE TIGER WHO ESCAPED

That tiger who, just for a lark,
Decided to quit Regents Park
When he first escaped,
The keeper just gaped,
It was midnight and foggy and dark.

Though lonely and frightened and cold,
That tiger was terribly bold,
He raised not a frown
As through Camden Town
He stalked, as in jungles of old.

Up steep Highgate Hill on his track,
(As of yore, did Dick Whittington's cat)
No longer a captive,
Alert, lithe and active,
Not once did that tiger look back.

At the 'Wellington' what a to-do,
Could this be his Waterloo?
For a fast panda car
Spotted him from afar,
And a very fast chase did ensue.

The end of this tale is bizarre,
Before they had got very far,
The tiger got worried,
And breathless and flurried
And was killed by a large *Jaguar.*

Barbara Shrubsole

FAMOUS LAST WORDS!

I'm going to diet
Really I am
I'm going to be skinny
Like Annie and Pam.

I'm going to get fit
And have plenty of go
I'm sure I can do it
The book told me so.

I'll get me a leotard
And some leggings to boot
Then I'll run and I'll skip
And I'll hop on one foot.

I'll jump up and down
Do exercises galore
With my feet in the air
And my head on the floor.

I'll count all the calories
Watch the sugar and fat
I'll skim all the milk
And give the cream to the cat.

I've got everything ready
All done and dusted
I feel tired out
Like a gut has been busted.

All that running around
Like a blue-tailed fly
I think I'll wait till tomorrow
To give it a try.

Jacqui Jones

THE DIBBLYDOO

Children, this poem is just for you
About a monster called the Dibblydoo
It has eight fingers and fourteen toes
And a rotting carrot for a nose.

It lurks about in the dead of night
Keeping out of everyone's sight
And when at last the moon goes down
He starts his journey into town.

And there he starts looking for his tea
Of boys and girls who have been naughty
When he finds them 'oh what a feast'
The horrible, slimy, horny beast.

Every single bite he savours
The naughtier the child the better flavour
Toes and fingers, arms and legs,
But best of all he likes their heads.

He eats their chest and their tums
And chews and gobbles at their bums,
And while the blood drips from his lips
He finishes off their bony hips.

Boys are bitter, girls are sweet
But everything goes including the feet
It needs just one and maybe two
To fill the tum of the Dibblydoo.

He likes them fat, he likes them thin
It doesn't matter what colour the skin,
He likes them big, he likes them small
It doesn't matter to him at all.

So there is one thing that you must do
To keep away from the Dibblydoo
Always behave as you should
Always, always you be *good.*

Denise Jeffcoate

LITTLE GREEN MAN

The little green man came up to town
And on his green face he wore a big frown
A Leprechaun he and on mischief bent
Like turning the milk and stealing the rent
Paddy McMurphy were waiting for he
And down his green trousers did put a big flea
He wriggled and jumped clear up to the moon
If he's ever back it will be too soon.

Dora Watkins

A Cat's Tale

The cat stopped in the roadway and glanced around
Seeing it was busy he sat down on the ground
As cars whizzed by he started licking his paws
Then stretched out full length and gaped his jaws.
He blinked in the sunshine at an approaching van
Then sat up and watched a delivery man.
He rolled on his back with his legs in the air
grabbed his tail - just because it was there.
He scratched his ears as a bike roared his way
Yawned as he watched the children at play.
He closed his eyes and flexed his toes
wrapped his tail round right up to his nose.
Suddenly he stiffened and dashed for his house
as around the corner scampered a tiny grey mouse!

Patricia Chilver

Loo Roll Lament

Why is it that in other bathrooms
Toilet rolls are there for all
While mine has always something missing
From that holder on the wall?

No tempting roll of coloured tissue,
Nothing left, to my despair,
Just a little tube of cardboard,
Brown and naked, hanging there.

No matter how I stock my cupboard
With a pile that's grand to see.
You may be sure it's always empty
When I need a roll for me!

I wonder if there's something lurking
In a corner, crouching, small,
And every time I change a loo roll
He darts out and eats it all?

If I ever turn to robbing
I know what my crime will be
No jewellery or antique heirlooms -
Loo roll nicking - that's for me!

For sometimes in a Ladies' Rest Room
Where the rolls are flowing free
I long to stuff some in my bag
To smuggle home for use *by me!*

Cynthia Briggs

A PAINFUL NIGHT

I life mine eyes unto the pills,
The ones the doctor left me.
Will they alleviate the pain
Which doth afflict me gravely?

To sit down here is not much fun -
Upstairs is such a bore.
And now the kitchen clock doth hum!
Whilst upstairs - thou dost snore!

I thump the clock, it stops the noise,
There's just my dog and me.
Now she's playing with her toys!
And it's only half-past *three!*

I J Wickert

DEAR MYSTIC MEG

Dear Mystic Meg, look into your crystal ball,
As of yet - I've had no luck at all,
I tune in every week to watch your sexy pout,
Dear Mystic Meg, please turn my luck about.

Dear Mystic Meg, I do two lines every Saturday,
Can't you manage to put a couple of bob this way?
When the moon is in Uranus and the stars are in your eyes,
Dear Mystic Meg, please give me a nice surprise.

Dear Mystic Meg, I'm not a greedy man,
I watch you every week, I'm your biggest fan,
Please will you do your best to make my dream come true,
Dear Mystic Meg, can I have your autograph *too ooo ooo!*

Martin Thompson

TURTLE FROLICS

Would you like to swim and frolic
Said the turtle to the crab
For I think our little pool
Is exceptionally drab

I think we would do better
To escape into the sun
We could have a big adventure
Play games and have some fun

We could lie about in deck chairs
Eating crisps and being fanned
While sipping champagne cocktails
And being very grand

I say old boy remember
Esmerelda getting caught
She was never very clever
So she landed in the pot

Well it didn't really suit her
She expected midnight blue
But the sauce they tried to serve her in
Was red and orange like glue

She almost screamed the place down
Till they brought some seafood dips
Then they garnished her with lettuce
And served her up with chips.

Evelyn Roxburgh

POETRY NOW

It was a year since he had sent
His work of art for punishment
He'd had a letter, typed in black
Which said they would be writing back

And patient should the writer be
And quietly wait his author's fee
At last a sound at his own door
Which somehow seemed to be, well, more

Than just a bill or letter from his sister
But truth to tell he hadn't missed her
A-cruising in the lusty Med
With newly wedded frightful Fred

With trembling fingers he did rape
The envelope, from its own shape
So large, imposing, grand and good
As publishers, do send, and could

At last this be the goal
Which he had aimed at: was his soul
And muse reward to find
O that the gods should be so kind

Dear Sir, he read, it is with joy
(He smiled and capered like a boy)
That we your royalty to you send
And hope, Sir, 'twill not be the end

Of endeavours which we like
A golden note we now must strike
We have enclosed your annual fee
It is one pound and pennies three.

He swore, he cried, cursed the amount
And then he tried to make the count
But only, stuck beneath the tape
He found a pound and penny shape

They'd done him down
He'd swore he'd crown
Their insolence he'd go one better
So Poetry Now - here is my letter!

Geoffrey Speechly

DAY TRIPPERS

Day trippers
Up and down the street
'Where's the best place to eat?
Mmm! Here. Hope there's a seat.'

Day trippers
Denture-slipping sippers
And dainty dippers
Of chocolate digestives

'We're from Dudley'
'Is all that for me?'
'Lovely cup of tea'
'And such nice crockery'

The till rings loudly
The tip box clunks proudly
With all the 20p's
Of appreciation

Day trippers
Swarming the town
Bargain hunting
Bags weighed down

Day trippers
Fifty thrifty over-fifties
Stampede to the coach like thunder
Onwards another town to plunder.

Vivienne M Wright

I'VE FALLEN OUT WITH MY MARROWS

I've fallen out with my marrows,
Will they ever get juicy and sound,
They're fed the right mixture,
But still plum-sized and glowering,
They hover just short of the ground.
Yes, I've fallen out with those meanies,
I don't think it's fair I've been blamed,
The cosseting they've had has been endless,
Yet they're acting as though they've been framed.
I've even been called an eccentric,
As I sometimes stay up all night long,
Just talking and coaxing, though they give me the pip,
Yes you'd think that I'd done something wrong.
I read up about them for ages,
As I've got this new gardening book,
I thought I'd done well, but they're giving me hell,
All I get is a hard acid look.
Yes, I've fallen out with my marrows,
But I won't go and turn them all loose,
As my book says they're known for their petulant moods,
So I'll let them stew in their own juice!

Jo Sparkes

A Very New Reporter

A very new reporter
Went searching for a scoop
His quarry drove straight at him
And made him loop the loop.

His slow recuperation
Provided ample leisure.
Of humour in a hospital
He wrote a goodly measure.

Partaking of a blanket-bath
- the best he'd had for ages
Pyjama pocket dipped in bowl
and pulped his precious pages.

One day, along the old grapevine
came, to our new reporter
A rumour that a surgeon famed
adored the cleaner's daughter.

And in an empty ward one day
He caught them both in bed:
But when he sought an interview
They threw him out, instead.

So now, our new reporter
is searching for a scoop
and seeks to gain a goodly fee
His losses to recoup.

Winifred Price

MIND GAMES

Was that a squeaking door I heard
Or just the night making a sound
I force myself to take a look
But there was nothing to be found

I hear the patter of tiny feet
Now I really start to worry
Or was it just a little mouse
Retreating in a hurry

Is that the window rattling
Or is someone rapping on the door
Should I go and investigate
Of this I'm not really sure

A figure of a man appears
It's only my shadow on the wall
Floorboards begin to creak
As I move on down the hall

Imagination has got the best of me
As I slowly make my way to bed
Are the stairs creaking behind me
Or was it all just in my head

The night had played its little tricks
There was nothing there to find
The darkness got the best of me
Played night games with my mind.

Roy Hunter

NATURE'S BALM

We strolled the woodland path,
The kids, Rusty and I:
Rusty ran, big branch in his mouth -
I had just thrown aside.

I watched and missed the sight
Of sludge, in front, and stuck fast
Clever kids held the branch tight
But I left my sandals behind

We used it again to reclaim them,
I had black, mud stockings on
Took a while to wash, upstream;
And Rusty behaved till we got home.

One time I followed the kids
Into a tunnel of shrubs.
Leaned, on down, with two sticks.
They snapped and hung my ponytail;

I swung from a branch as they laughed
While the pain of scalping grew;
No question as to the fact
Nature's got it in for me . . .

L Linton

THE FLY AND THE DISH

A fly on the wall is most annoying,
When with another fly, it is toying;
Buzzing here and buzzing there,
With little thought, with little care;
Spreading germs where'er it lands,
Picked up by my delicately, manicured hands;
Germs invisible to the naked eye,
But if swallowed, My! . . . Oh . . . My!

My fly swatter I deftly swing,
I'll make that fly's earhole ring;
Swish! . . . I'll get that devil fly,
Drat! . . . Knocked over the apple pie;
Swish! . . . Here goes again,
Drat! . . . Knocked out the window pane;
Swish! . . . I'll get that devil fly,
Missed again, I'll have another try;
Swish! . . . *Drat!* . . . Hit the light bulb instead,
Blamed thing landed on my head;
A nasty cut I do perceive,
For blood is dripping down my sleeve.

The flies, well they don't really care,
Blamed thing's settled in my hair;
'Hit it dear, when I say ready,
Any time now dear. Steady! Steady!'
I may feel pain a bit intense,
But that devil fly will pay recompense.
'No Dear!' . . . That's not the fly swatter.'
Swish! . . . 'That's a D . . . I . . . Shhhhh!'

H Parker

OOPS A DAISY

The teardrops, on her lashes, shone like diamonds in the sun,
Nothing I could say, could undo what had been done,
I said I did not ever think, that you and I, could ever part this way
She shrugged her shoulders, as if there was, nothing more to say.
Just a little while ago, we were so close, we were as one,
Just one spoken word, and all the magic there, was gone,
All my pleading for forgiveness, and apologies, in vain,
For in the heat of passion, I had called my 'Sally', *Jane!*.

Albo

THE RACE

The Boss arrived that morning, in the brand new shiny Jag,
The building site was silent, as he climbed out with his bag,
The lads all crowded round it, asking just what it could do,
'Over a ton' he told them, 'this car will certainly move.'
But one young fellow stood there, visibly unimpressed,
'This is only a motor, and this model isn't the best,
And if you will cover a tenner, to gamble on its looks,
I'll race you five miles to the village, and me in wellington boots.'
The Boss could not be chicken, in front of all his crew,
'All right' he said, 'you're on then, I'll have that ten off you,'
The young lad took his coat off, and turned upon his heel,
'I'll wait for you in the village, you and your fancy wheels.'
And then he started running out of the muddy site,
And the Boss jumped in his treasure, and snapped the seatbelt tight,
But now as he came to the village, he gave a startled shout,
Cars were over and burning, and two shop window blown out,
He stopped and asked a local, if there had been civil war,
'The like of this' the local said 'I've never seen before.
A geezer came racing in here, he must have been doing a ton,
Had a blow-out in one of his wellies, we can't seem to find
                              where he's gone!'

Charles H Boyett

HALLELUJAH

A young lady lived down our way
Who spoke very crudely all day.
A sudden conversion
Killed off the perversion
But left her with little to say.

Stephen R Ramsden

WHEN I GET OLD

When I get old, don't pity me.
Don't make me go to bed too early
With endless cups of tea.
Don't shake your head and sigh,
And squeeze my shoulders comfortingly
As you pass by.

Make me feel as young as I want to feel.
Make me do things for myself.
Let me imagine I'm in good health.
Compliment me on my looks.
Buy me naughty videos,
And romantic books.

And if my mind begins to roam,
Please don't put me in a Home,
Unless it's with an elderly,
Wealthy, sexy man.
Then, I think,
Maybe you can . . .

Betty Walton

DON'T TREAD IN IT!

I love the doggy population - but
often think that as a nation -
We need to get our priorities right,
Recognise their owners can be a blight.
Don't 'hear me wrong' - as I come
on strong - All that those owners
must do is deal with pets' 'pooh!'
Not leave it there for all to share.

Patricia Lawrence

FUNNY FARM

Yes,
they'll take you away
to the funny farm
The one just over the hill
there they'll strap you up
in a padded coat
and feed you
little red pills.
And if you get
too lonely
or go as loony
as can be
they'll throw you in
a padded cell
Then forget
where they put the key
Yes
Forget where they put
the *key*.

A J Marshall

THE MOTORIST'S PRAYER

Well here I go again,
Finding fault with the ways of men.
But 'tis always the soft option see,
For me to blame you; and not me.

That man ahead in jets should be,
Poor fool seeks eternity.
The one behind has got no light;
Poor dad's uptight with fright.

Up ahead it's old Joe Bloggs;
Yesterday he nearly popped his clogs.
Left is right to Joe you see;
Never mind leave him be.

Liz has joined the motorway;
Now's the time for all to pray.
Vicar in old three-wheeler;
For such are the ways of men,
Got dog in back again.

Now I see the district nurse,
All behind please like a hearse.
Up ahead AA and RAC
They've seen it all before you see.

People just like you and me;
Perhaps burdened with anxiety.
Alright then, they've made you sigh;
But people can make you laugh and cry.

Next time you fault your fellow men;
Then add yourself to them.

                              Amen.

W Hopkins

THE BLACK CAT

The black cat fell in the bucket
as the man was mixing cement
He threw the water on the mixing
and the cat turned out like a tent!

The man looked down in horror
as it tried to straighten out . . .
I wish it was tomorrow
with the cat just running about!

Get out the hosepipe, turn on the tap
before the cement overlaps!
Let the water flow like torrential rain
then the cat will be meowing again!

Marie Barker

JIM RETIRES

This world the day is aa gan wrang fin ye hae a good look roon,
I'm sure in twenty years or so, there'll nae be tradesmen in the toon.
So dinna think yer time's been wasted, dinna think it's been in vain,
We the kind o wirk that's deen the day, hooses winna be the same.

When yer wirkin days have clean run oot, noo dinna sit an greet,
Pit aa yer tools up on the shelf, sit doon pit up yer feet.
Bit dinna sit for ower lang, for it's nae guid for the body,
Jist has a think on fit tae dee and find yersel a hobby.

I widnae recommend the drinkin, it be a gie expensive wye,
Although wie some folk noo a days, it seems to be the cry.
The game o golf is nae sae bad bit I ken it's nae for you,
And I've tried the game of bowls masel, an I'm dammed if
                                                    they'll run true.

Some days ye'll hae time on yer hands, so think aboot yet wishes,
And turn yer hand tae your guid wife and help her wie the dishes.
I ken that she's been guid tae you in a the years geen by,
And though hoosework's nae yer style, ye could aye geet a try.

Fit ever ye wid like tae dee, an I'm sure ye'll hae been scheemin,
And if ye'd like tae live a while, then forget aboot the weemin.
So my advice tae you wid be, just dinna be a feel,
And find yersel a jobbie like the eens ye dee sae weel.

We wish ye a the very best and hae a fling the night,
There's naething like a wee bit dram for a guid auld fassioned vright.
So look ahead on times tae come and never mind the wither,
And some night nae sae far awa we'll hae a dram thegither.

Many happy years to come,
Freda and Sandy.

Sandy

A GRAVE OCCASION

During the processional hymn
When the nave lights were all dim,
A choirgirl's heel stuck in a grating
But she marched on without one shoe . . .
The following choirboy of chivalry rating
Picked up both shoe and grating!
Whereupon the vicar promptly fell
Into the hole below . . .
Somewhat changing the content of
                    his intoning
To the surprise of the old ladies
Who learning some strange new words
Stored them to talk of them
                    during future phoning!

L J Crockford

ONLY A SPLINTER

There was a time when I was young
I had this huge great splinter
Stuck deep inside my bum.
I was taken to the hospital
Where I was a source of fun.
The staff thought it amusing
I'd got a splinter in my bum
They put me on a table
Turned a spotlight on full glare.
I heard the nurses tittering
At the weird case in their care
They probed around my bottom
Till they got the splinter out
But compared to the embarrassment
My splintered bum was nowt!

Gordon Barnett

THE SALAD

Why is it, when I mention salad,
boring lettuce comes to mind.
With a tomato here, and a radish there,
it takes a lot combined
To make a good and tasty meal,
with which the family will feel
full to the brim and satisfied,
And not look at the plate, like
                    everything's just died.
To use the unusual things I find,
like fruit and veg of all kinds.
Anything goes into my salad,
whatever I decide.
I sit and devise, my ingredients by my side.
In my kitchen, with oils and dressings galore
I concoct a salad
That makes them shout for more.

Sandra Houghton

WOMEN DRIVERS!

He believes in equality
But things can go too far,
He doesn't think a woman
Is fit to drive a car.

He wants to hurry home,
Have a beer and watch TV,
But there's a single line of traffic
As far as one can see.

A woman is in front of him
And wouldn't you just know,
She's keeping to the MPH
And that is far too slow.

Over in the other lane
There is a mile-long queue,
Someone needs a right-hand turn
She stops to let her through.

As he sits there fuming
He knows what he will do,
He will drive onto the shoulder
And pass that 'You know who.'

He will not stay behind her,
He has to take a chance,
And now he has the speed he craves,
He's in a ambulance.

B C Watts

SUPERMARKET NIGHTMARE

'Can we have some crisps Mam?'
'What about these?'
'Chocolate biscuits, wow, yes please.'
'Put them all back'
you hear yourself say
'I'm trying to do my shopping
now just walk nice and
don't go away.'
'Don't climb on the trolley
Don't run in the aisles
Mind you don't knock that lady'
The manager's all smiles.
Your brain becomes empty
now where is that list?
Oh where have I put it
I'm going round the twist.
'One of you fetch the beans
I'll get the bread'
The youngest one's gone missing
this is what I dread
I see him at the checkout
'Just choosing sweets' he says
I drag him back to the trolley
then we are on our way
'Don't squash the yoghurts
don't break the jam
just stay with the shopping
I'll fetch the ham.
Now which pop would you like kids
oh don't bother I'll just choose
You're both there pulling faces
And I am not amused.
I know you're fed up of shopping
Well let's be on our way
I haven't got all I wanted
I'll get it another day.

A day when I'm not hassled
When you don't drive me mad
'cos the pair of you aren't coming
you're staying with your Dad.

Angela Brown

TRIBUTE TO RED DWARF

Oh Arnold Rimmer, what's happened to you
Dave Lister has got you in a bit of a stew
You're no longer a living breathing man
Now you're a smegging hologram.
'Rimsey and Listy' when you want something done
You treat young Dave like a long-lost son
But it isn't long before he gets you annoyed
And soon you're calling him 'Goit' and 'Gimboid'.
How can you put up with Holly
Deadpan computer who is sometimes jolly
Then there's the Cat, a creature so rare
Crumple his suits, if you dare.
Then Holly disappeared and in his place
Along came Kryten old tin-face
And if you thought you had troubles before
Now you've got them by the score.
Oh, there *is* Holly, whatever next?
For Holly's gone and changed his sex
He's now a woman and no longer clever
Can't even tell a change in the weather.
But Arnold Rimmer, you're the best
Keeping fit in shorts and vest
Please never ever dock in the wharf
Carry on moaning aboard Red Dwarf.

Susan Gordon

THE KIPPER

The kipper is a versatile fish
You can serve it for breakfast
Or your main evening dish
It's very tasty alongside afternoon tea
With your old friend the kipper you're never at sea

The kipper is a traditional fish
Eaten by Churchill
It was his dying wish
To have a large kipper for his evening meal
Enriched with some mustard and a cutlet of veal

The kipper is an intelligent fish
If you heed its advice
Then in time you'll grow rich
It knows all about money, emeralds and gold
Have you ever seen a kipper-run company fold?

The kipper is an athletic fish
It can swim in marathons
Without getting a stitch
In gymnastic prowess it's the king of the sea
All the young mermaids cry, 'It's a kipper for me!'

The kipper's majestic
Let the kipper swim free
Though I hope that my eulogy
Doesn't sound twee
May its song be eternal
Pray the species stays strong
For with our ally the kipper
You can never ever
Well very rarely ever
Go wrong.

Stuart Delvin

ITS VISIT

At 'its' urgent knock I opened the door,
It scrambled in, and swirled the floor,
Swept over the windows, smothered the grate,
Slurping and shuddering with heaving weight.
It painted the walls with bilious trails,
Then writhed across to the banister rails.
Clinging with zest it revved up speed and
Zoomed upstairs for a ravenous feed.
It oozed the bed, and munched the tele,
All was devoured into its belly.
Vivid green and spotted pink, it drummed
A tattoo on the bathroom sink.
With one tremendous eddy it whirled,
Through the door, and there unfurled,
A feathered crest of colours bright,
Then hurtled away, into the night.
Onwards it scurried into the rain -
I hope 'it' never calls here again!

Catherine Whyley

WHIMSICAL WIT

It happened in a dream
I ate some blue ice-cream.
Then a cat with many tails
Did a dance of seven veils.
A policeman in a punt
Wore his tunic back to front.
There were rabbits in a line
Drinking elderberry wine
And a rather sprightly goat
In a pale blue overcoat.
But I felt the final straw
Was the notice on the door
'No need to be shy -
Judgement Day is nigh -
So please remove your coat
And be prepared to vote!
Do *not* shout or scream -
This is a private dream'

No more 'plonk' for me
I think I'll stick to tea!

Doreen Conway-Haynes

ONE AT A TIME ON THE SCALES

I've shaved my armpits
Clipped all long nails
Had my hair cut
But there's no kidding
                    The scales!

Ann Weavers

PRIDE BEFORE A FALL

I really am so houseproud
I love to mop my floors
I dust in every corner
Even check the top of doors
My home is looking perfect
Hubby's a wizard with his drill
But soon there may be chaos here
I forgot to take my pill!

Christina Lindsay

ARACHNAPHOBIA

I am a great big spider
With eight long hairy legs -
My web is attached to a clothesline
On which hangs a bag of pegs.

I trap all sorts of insects
Sometimes an ant or bug
Then wrap them all in gossamer
To keep 'em nice and snug!

My nightmare happened wash-day
Whilst basking in the sun
As a lady hung her smalls out
My home came all undone.

The swinging made me dizzy
She gave one yell then fled
Haven't seen her since '*Thank God*'
She tumble-dries instead!

Marion Lawson

TOMMY'S TEA

Sitting by the river
Tommy ate his tea
along came a spider
but Tommy didn't see
he sat down beside Tommy
looking in glee
he knew that very soon
he'd be eating Tommy's tea
he crawled up Tommy's leg
and sat down on his plate
Tommy jumped up
but it was too late
the spider was very hungry
he gobbled Tommy's tea
and all that Tommy could do
was stand by and see.

Linda Casey

JASPER!

Years ago, living in a Tipton street!
A man named Jasper, my brother went to meet.
Now this old guy, was an old fashioned sort.
He would sell his own mother, if she could be bought.

Knocking on his door, 'Tap, tap, tap.'
Out he pops, wearing his grandad cap.
'What do you want, he says with a gruff scowl.
At the side of his legs, a dog starts to growl.

'Have you got any 'bikes' for sale?
His face softens up, and the dog wags his tail!
'How much can you afford kid?'
'My dad just gave me fifteen quid.'

The rusty bike in the corner, caught my brother's eye.
Pushing it around the side of the house, feeling on a high!
There he was, standing by the gate!
'Fifteen quid, and it's yours mate!'

Sitting in the saddle, free-wheeling down the street.
The front wheel falls out, and the street and his face meet.
Jasper doesn't care, he's got the cash.
Relaxing in front of the television, surrounded by trash.

For years after, I have seen children that are poor.
With goods in their hands, banging on his door.
You don't see many characters like this any more!

L M Pearson

UNTITLED

There was a young man went to Leeds,
What he really went for were some seeds
A pot plant or two,
Or anything new
You see he was a do-it-yourself man.
So he drove down the lane,
But all was in vain
He could not find a DIY shop.
Then out of the blue,
A man came in view
He got out of his van
And said, 'Excuse me my man,'
But is there a B & Q in Leeds.
The man with good deeds
Said, 'Well at a guess'
'I'd say there was an L two EEs a D and an S.'

Joan Fathers

SWEATED LABOUR

His master worked him like a slave
for just a pittance
And kept him working till the stroke
Of five o'clock, nor ever gave
A thought toward his comfort.
He staggered under bales
Of straw or bags of flour,
Then fetched the milk, 'ere it was sour,
To feed the kittens.
He carried heavy pails
Of various liquids back and fore.
Sometimes the loads he bore
Were so inhuman.
Four bucketfuls of white of eggs
His master called albumen;
Enough to buckle both his legs;
Slung on a pole that almost broke
His back - And that's no yolk!

G Aldsmoor

DUMPY

My trousers help to swell my shape
Round and dumpy like a grape.
I do not gorge, I do not glut,
So why do I have difficulty in covering my gut?
I try day after day
To wobble it away.
But it's of no use for it stays
When I walk, it does sway.
It is such a shock
That people mock.
Folk especially the blokes
Treat my shape of a grape as a joke.
I don't have a waist
I am so shame-faced.
I eat the least, I never feast
Why do I look like such a fat beast?
It's the same with my chest
'Favourably blessed,'
And what of my hips?
As big as my lips
With which I blow a kiss:
Corpulent crisis!

Denise Shaw

SNEEZY BEE?

Whilst others dream of glorious summer sun
I think of pollen-itchy eyes and streaming nose,
and I wonder if bees
ever sneeze.

Veronica Stanway

F P BONES

When Uncle Jerry became Auntie Joan,
My grandmother cried,
My cousin left home,
At work he was ridiculed then given the sack,
But Joan didn't mind or ever look back,
You see my friends had a band they called the coin,
Joan played the guitar like Hendrix so had to join,
From that day on they shot to fame,
Things for my dress wearing uncle were never the same,
She went to look after homeless children in Spain,
I get a postcard now and again,
My dad thinks his brother has gone insane,
But I tell him again and again,
The world would be boring if we were all the same.

Kevin Axon

BATTLE OF THE FOOTBALL STICKERS

There occurs a metamorphosis, it happens every year,
When friendships loose all meaning, and football's all you hear,
When common sense is lost to you; you fear you've gone insane,
Mark my words, I know those signs, it's sticker time again!
And so begins my story of a friendship now not pure,
Brought down by football albums (And I'm told there is no cure)
It started with one sticker; just one row between our sons,
But then quickly escalated into battle of the mums.
Our lives since then have changed a lot, just waiting for the words,
'Premier League is out again! In case you have not heard!'
Grab my purse then off I go, the shop knows me by name,
And I get there in a time that would make Gazza cry in shame.
Then standing in the playground, with a semblance of calm,
I spot her in the distance with her album under arm,
Our eyes lock 'cross the playground and she makes the sign for tea,
Our show-down has arrived and from now on it's her or me.
Our talk it starts as usual with the giants of the field,
And then goes in more detail to their advantageous build.
Then with a grin, the words at last, 'A look before you leave?'
That leaves me in no doubt that she's an ace hid up her sleeve.
It's Arsenal first, and fear grips hard, she can't have him, I'll wage,
But David Seaman smiles at me - from *her* album page.
I force an icy smile and choke back words that don't befit,
And clamping tears that fill my eyes, I say, 'You jammy person!'
So page by page our duel goes on, 'You'll find I've David Platt'
'Well I've got Jordi Cruyff and it's a shiny one at that!'
'Ravenelli, Cantona, Vinnie Jones and Shearer,
Schmeichel, Giggs, Vialli, I've also got Asprilla!;
Then when finally she left me, I was not the one to cry,
As she failed to see the scissors, I'm afraid that caught my eye . . .

Debbie Neal

THE LITTLE GERBIL

The little gerbil ran in his wheel
Then he stopped waiting still.
Catching his breath, twitching his nose
Pumping his feet to end the pose.

His spindly legs taking the strain.
His tiny muscles fighting the pain.
His body kept in perfect trim
Just in case admirers drop in.

Colin Farmer

MAGS CAF

If you want a good nosh but cheap in price,
I can show you a place it's simple but nice.
There's food in abundance it's all piping hot,
And always plenty of tea in the pot.
The woman in charge is a serious cook,
If you eat there on Saturdays it's better to book.
Her scones are to die for and so is her stew,
There's always second helpings too.
The opening hours are early till late,
And when you arrive you are handed a plate.
The question then asked is what will it be,
You could stay there for breakfast lunch and tea.
Where is this you ask for there are no others,
It's quite simple really it's round at my mother's.

Ali Martin

A GRITTY SNOWMAN

There's not much you can do with two inches of snow
but my grandson thought he would 'have a go'
at building a snowman nevertheless
but how it would turn out is anyone's guess.

He called up his friend to carry out his mission
as in the old 'winter tradition!'
They had to work hard as the sun came out
soon there would be even less snow about.

With fingers turned numb, scraping at what
they could find
true enough, you could call it a snowman of
'some kind' . . . only,
this one would not win a prize, forget the shape
'Look at the size'

The poor little 'Icy Gent' looked more like
some heap of cement!
In desperation, quite frustrated, dirt, grass
and stones were incorporated
You have to work hard when the sun melts it all
but these two little boys, were having a *ball!*

Maria Johanna Gibbs

CANNY CANINE

I wish I were of human breed,
I'd ditch the collar and the lead.
No more 'Walkies!', No more 'Sit!',
No more obeying clueless twit.
Sure, I've got a friendly home,
Comfy bed in the lobby,
But I do resent the need to roam
Outdoors for every 'jobby'.

I wish I were of human breed,
Then I would learn to talk and read.
I'd be too old to go to school,
So, just like 'Master', I would drool
Over cuties, daily on Page Three.
Yes, - that sounds the life for me!
I'd wave 'goodbye' to fetching sticks
And doing all those silly tricks.
A gourmet diet I would chose
And p'raps I'd even learn to booze!
No longer would I have to chase
Next door's cat then turn and race
That stuck up bitch from Number Eight
To check the postman at her gate.
No more growling at each stranger
Or warning barks at hint of danger.
Oh yes, a human I'd wish to be,
Unchained, unhindered, completely free
To plan my future, examine life,
Maybe, even take a wife.
But, speaking as a humble dog
Who's oft been thwarted in mid snog,
The hazard I most need to miss
Above all else, is simply this -
The twit advancing with pail of water
Whilst I'm beguiling someone's daughter!

Geoffrey C Lee

BUS STOP LAUGHTER

Standing at the bus stop, I heard a lady say
'I've been here 90 minutes, is there another bus today?'
There'll be one here quite soon dear, which number were you after?
And when I heard her answer, I filled the air with laughter.

'Have they all got numbers? I didn't realise.
I just waited for a colour that was pleasing to the eyes.
I didn't like the red one, it looks so old and shabby.
I didn't fancy yellow, it had a lady cabby.
So I thought I'd hang around a while. I suppose you think I'm dotty.
But I'm waiting for another one - either striped or spotty.'

Pam Brown

EVERY DOG HAS ITS DAY!

Now William gathered all his troops
To fight the Hastings war.
He fancied Harold's crown and throne.
He'd not been King before!

His men were mostly large and tall
And they looked pretty fit,
So William rubbed his hands in glee
And thought 'Yes, this is it!'

He spoke to one who said 'My Duke,
Just see me swing this axe!
Those Englishmen will bite the dust.
I'll stop them in their tracks!'

The next man said 'I'll do you proud!
I'm expert with the spear.
One sight of me, I'm telling you
Will fill them all with fear!'

The Duke espied a tiny man
Who spoke quite timidly.
'I am a bowman if you please.
They will be scared of me!'

But William, filled with doubt said next
'Well, prove how good you are.'
The arrows went all round the field
And landed near and far!

'My little man' the Duke then said.
'On you I can't rely.
The way you shoot you might well hit
Some poor chap in the eye!'

John Christopher

'AT LAST' A FRESH WIND ON MAY 1ST

The parliamentary wind blows hard with greed and sleaze
As many full sails unfold to catch all of the breeze
Totally impervious to big waves and rocks
Politicians have more faces than Town Hall clocks
Unlike Cinderella they won't leave at twelve
For more treasure trove they continue to delve.
The back door remains open for all those that flop
As they hurriedly leave the 'Good Ship Lollipop'
Parting Westminster they flex their political muscles
Once aboard 'Le Shuttle' it's straight off to Brussels.
Or back to the City behind the barricade
Safely protected by the 'Old Boys' brigade
Welcomed by Merchant Bankers and big city combinations
As useful 'lobby fodder', for sale to many Eastern Nation.
For those of declining years. The Upper House is seen by many
As a quick afternoon snooze, to earn on honest penny
Thus rested and refreshed it's off to the club
For port or claret combined with good grub
So everybody can always start again, back on board the gravy train
With plenty perks and privileges for their own personal gain.

John Scott

PIGMANIA

Be gentle to the pig
Let him hear you sing,
Admire his complexion
Talk to him of spring.

A pig can be a friend
Notice those tiny feet,
Just made for jogging -
Line-dancing down the street.

If you have a home
With a room to spare,
Buy a trough today
Show him that you care.

Maureen Macnaughtan

HANDY TAM

Ma man thinks he's brilliant.
Jist take the ither day:
He went tae mow the front lawn:
The grass as high as hay.

He wore his carpet slippers,
A thing he should not do.
The Flymo sliced the cable:
He ruined his slippers too.

A very lucky man are you,
I screeched with angry voice.
Ach weel ah'll buy a new pair,
Says he, so jist rejoice.

I planted rows of lettus seeds:
Green blades showed, tiny size.
He took the hoe and weeded them.
Left none, to win a prize.

I went to prune the roses:
No secateurs could see,
So, ah better shut ma mooth noo,
Before he murders me.

C Shanks

ME

I turn from the mirror I don't want to see the scrawny old woman that
used to be me,
Inside I'm the same but the packaging's changed, I hate being shut in
this skinny old frame,
Where are the thick glossy tresses of gold the soft silky skin now
wrinkled and old,
What happened to the body so shapely and round these days it droops
almost down to the ground,
I totter around on these spindly old legs they won't run any more they
look more like pegs,
The bright sparkling eyes so big and so blue have to wear silly specs
to see who is who,
When I sleep I dream I am having such fun I laugh and I dance as
I used to when young,
The shock is severe when you wake up and find the dreams you've
been dreaming are all in your mind,
Quite often I forget I am old you see, and when I look in the mirror
I expect to see me.

Muriel Burgess

GRANDAD SPIDER

Grandad's got this spider
tattooed on 'is 'ead
he used to be really 'ard
that what granny spider said.

He wears a greying toupee
there's a cobweb underneath
he keeps it by his bedside
right next to his teeth.

He used to ride a motorbike
everyone feared his name
now he's the terror of the old folk's home
on his hot rod walking frame.

D Morley

TROUBLE IN THE BOILERHOUSE

Things are going badly in the boilerhouse.
The rottweilers are on the loose.
They've killed the foreman and fed the mouse
and now they're after the goose.

Things are not good in the boilerhouse.
The tea bags have gone to pot,
the rottweilers have eaten the biscuits
and all the boilers have blown their top.

Things are getting worse in the boilerhouse.
The social workers are moving in
They've taken away all the stokers
and chucked the rottweilers in the bin.

Things can't get worse in the boilerhouse
for the boilers have all exploded.
The mouse chewed through the fail safe device
and so they became overloaded.

Things are looking up in the boilerhouse.
The rottweilers seem almost appealing
The social workers brought back the stokers
and the goose has flown up to the ceiling.

The shift will end soon in the boilerhouse.
Then we'll set the rottweilers free;
the goose can come down from the ceiling;
and we'll get a good cup of tea.

Janis Priestley

Baby's Hat

Who gave him that silly hat?
Who placed it on his head?
He's looking rather chirpy now
because he's just been fed
he'll only be a baby
for just a little while
so we'll keep taking photos
just look at his cute smile.

J Benford

ARACH-NO-PHOBIA?

A very hairy spider was sitting in my bath -
I screamed and ran away from him, but all he did was laugh

His legs were long and twiddly . . . they took up all the room
I dashed off to the kitchen to find a deadly broom

I tiptoed in that place again to squash him in the plughole -
The sneaky thing had vanished, to thank me for my trouble

I heard him trundle down the hall; he sounded like a lorry
I crept up on him broom and all - yes, I would make him sorry

He turned around and looked at me and scrunched into a ball
His eyes shone with a dewy plea - I couldn't do it after all

So he and I we are now friends, I will not kill another -
And hoping I can make amends, I treat him like a brother.

Deborah Banks

A BUMP IN THE NIGHT

Semi-conscious the other night
awakened yes with such a fright.
A bump or bang what can it be?
It didn't sound too far from me.
Again I hear that sudden noise,
what can it be? There is no voice.
Inside I think the sound does come
once more I hear - oh I'm so numb.
Senses return a little bit
yes now I see so up I sit.
Ah silly me it's quite all right
along the landing out of sight
behind a door so firmly shut
just someone snoring loud tut, tut.

Margaret Jackson

OUT FOR A ROW

A friend and I we hired a boat,
didn't know much except it would float,
We each took an oar and began to row,
One went one way, the other don't know,
round and round we seemed to spin,
getting nowhere fast and couldn't win,
the current took us down the river,
a wind got up, we began to shiver,
I became so stiff and could hardly move,
We changed seats with an oar out of groove,
Some water came in and we were stuck,
if we sank now, would just be our luck,
We moved around, the boat up tipped,
I turned and saw my coat had ripped,
We headed back in quite a state,
lost all track of time, only an hour late!

R Ellis

WORLD WAR II IS OVER - TELL HIM, SOMEONE!

The siren sounds at the workshop
As it did thirty years ago,
Though then it was sounds of wartime,
Old Harold still thinks it is so.
He lives in the past with his memoirs,
Embroiders brave deeds he has done,
Half-heartedly flicks with his chamois,
The tasks of the day not begun.
His enemies circle around him
In his cosy watch-tower base -
The sparrows are chirruping shrapnel
And threaten his pin-up's face.
His window-periscope's broken,
Against ammunition no foil,
Now crows in Luftwaffe formation
Drop incendiaries in general turmoil.
The pigeons are plotting together
With rats from the underground;
The heater is hissing out poisonous gas -
Can't move till the 'all clear' should sound!
He sits with a smoke and a cuppa
And contemplates great gallant deeds;
Oh, Harold, you've told us a whopper,
You were only a ragman in Leeds!
Trembling, he lays his face downward
As he hears aircraft drones overhead.
It's a holiday flight to the Island of Wight,
Please tell him or he'll shoot them all dead!
You've had a hard day, poor old Harold,
Though your working tools lie there untouched,
It's Victory Day for Great Britain,
With you keeping the enemy watched.

Oh, won't someone please go and tell him,
Though the truth will hit terribly hard,
That victory was won fully thirty years gone,
And the boss is coming up with his card!

Evelyn Friend

THE DREADED LURGY

I had a wretched virus, which made me feel quite ill
I needed no persuasion to lie down - or be still
My body ached all over, my skin was even sore
The sight of food repulsed me - each movement was a chore
The doctor came - he looked at me, checked my chest and back
'Sorry you've got a virus, can't give you anything for that'
He had to rush away quickly, but just had time to say
'No food, just fluids for awhile, you'll soon be well again'
And, sure enough as time went by, progress was being made
Only slowly I must admit, but I wasn't looking so grey
So! If you have a virus, don't bother to all your doctor
Just curl up in a nice warm bed, and stay there till you're stronger
Having had this virus I can guarantee, that eventually it *will* go
But do not get impatient, for its passing is quite slow
PS I forgot to mention, it leaves you with a cough
And if there's no medication, the going gets pretty rough.

Fran Merrett

ENGLISH AS SHE IS SPOKE

We English speak plain English,
But consider this my friend.
If it's not your native language,
It can be hard to comprehend.

Some of our English idioms,
Aren't easy to understand,
If you happen to be a foreigner,
From some distant foreign land.

Like when we say we are 'fed up',
A foreigner might think,
We always have to go upstairs,
To get our food and drink.

Other things we like to say,
Can be distinctly iffy.
Whatever would a Frenchman make,
Of a phrase like 'in a jiffy?'

And if you should say, 'It's left behind,'
Or 'It's right behind you chum.'
A foreigner could then suppose,
You're referring to your bum.

Gerry Boxall

COMIC CAPERS

A certain young man from Nepal
Had quite a serious fall;
With no parachute
He took the fast route,
While sky-diving down in Bengal.

Another young man from Nepal
Also had quite a fall,
It dented the pride
Of this fine mountain guide -
But it dented his head most of all.

Sam Stafford

I Wish

I wish I could be thinner
Trouble is I like my dinner
Sausages, pies, potatoes of every sort
Chocolate bars I wish I'd never bought
Drinks I guzzle instead of taking sips
Wow look at the size of my hips
Every part of me has started to wobble
due to food I love to gobble
the only way I can get thin
Is if someone pricks me with a pin.

Terry Knight

TWO FARMING FRIENDS

A question asked by Farmer Green
To Brown his dearest friend
My foal it has a common cold
What do you recommend?

My horse last summer had a cough
This mix he drank like wine.
A home-made brew of alcohol
Meth spirit and turpentine.

Farmer Green departed then
And drove home to his farm
Gave his foal the wonder mix
Protecting it from harm.

At morning light young Farmer Green
Arrived at stable door
Greeted by four upright hooves
Foal dead upon the floor

Farmer Green phoned Farmer Brown
Bad crackling on the line
Shouting that his foal had died
Reply was 'So did mine.'

B Anderson

DEVIOUS

His eyes were navy blue,
I melted beneath their gaze.
Who was he? This wonderful creature,
I was in a daze.

I needed to know him,
I was fascinated.
Please, oh God let him speak to me,
Or I will be truly devastated.

He took my hand,
I almost swooned.
Was it a 'Fatal attraction?'
Was I doomed?

I was so excited,
And he seemed delighted.
But how devious men can be,
He just wanted to share a taxi with me.

Mabel Barber

UNTITLED

Little Jack Horner
Sat in a corner
Nursing a bottle of rye,
Compelled to pause
For a while because
He'd drunk two others dry.

K D Savell

THE DROUGHT

Must cut down on water
Is something we're all told,
Doesn't matter if it's hot
Or if it's extremely cold.

You must never waste it
There isn't much about,
So that means no more hosing
Of that there is no doubt.

Pack your rubber ducks away
Baths will get the push,
No more water going down
The plug hole with a whoosh.

Boys will all give a grin
When covered in mud and dirt,
Only one thing bothers them
Water pistols that won't squirt!

Maureen Daniel

A QUESTION OF CLOTHES

With boys wearing long, flowing locks
and girls sporting short, shingled crops
and wearing ties
and trews with flies.
We have concern for those
in unisex clothes.
Do I sigh for the days
when women wore stays,
Oh no.
All I ask is to know
when I give up my seat on a bus,
Is it one of them?
Or one of us?

Muriel Reed

SCHOOL ROLL CALL

At 8.45 my Close comes alive
The peace and quiet is shattered,
A small retreat
All tidy and neat
Fills with cars, some new, some battered.

They come from the right, reverse from the left,
Jockey to get the best places;
Drive over the kerb,
That one's a right 'erb!
He thinks it's the sports car races.

Daily they come bringing children to school,
Pedestrians find them daunting.
I'm a high jumper
Missing a bumper
When driving skills they are flaunting.

E Balmain

LAST BUS HOME

Saturday night I go to the Legion
Meet up with my old friend,
A couple of pints and a chinwag,
It cheers both of us up no end.

I pop next door to the chip shop,
Fish and chips, mushy peas in a tub,
Off to catch the last bus home,
It stops right outside our club.

Last Saturday I queued behind a man and his wife,
Their eight or nine children too,
The mother and her children boarded the bus
The driver then shouts, sorry I'm full, that will have to do.

It's a two mile walk home for me,
My fish and chips, mushy peas, will be cold,
Two miles is not very far when you're young
Different for me with my bad leg and I'm getting old.

The children's father and I start walking,
My walking stick tap, tapping the ground,
Your sticks tapping is most annoying he said
As he looked down his nose and frowned.

Can you not stop that irritating noise,
Do you have to tap your walking cane,
Having to walk home is bad enough without your stick tap, tapping,
On and on he moaned, he was being a right old pain.

Why have you not put a rubber on the end of your stick,
That was it, I'd had enough of his childish fuss,
So I told him had he bothered to put one on his,
We could have been on the last blooming bus!

Frederick Sowden

THE FLY

Can anyone tell me the reason why,
There is need for the existence of a fly.
This really irksome little pest,
Builds neither home burrow or nest
Nor does it build a web and dangle,
But merely flies off at some odd angle
To avoid being swatted eaten or chewed,
Or something just as disgusting or crude.
Each day we see them flying around the air
Each of us allotted our own fair share.
I think in the beginning, when God has finished man
And the rest of the animals he had began,
There remained a speck of matter that caught his eye,
And not being wasteful he made a fly.

Jack Ellis

IN DAYS OF OLD

In days of old,
When knights were bold,
and women were big and busty,
The gigolos wore armour but -
parts of it went rusty!

Beth Jackson

ITCHY SAGA

I am a flea
The best there can be,
Adept at irritation.
Flea collars send
Me to t'other end
Evasive situation.
When my host sleeps,
I practise leaps,
Maximum aggravation.
When they try a bath
I merely laugh,
Change my location.
I am a flea,
Breed fast as can be
Explosive population.
Spray gave a puff,
That was enough . . .
Final exhalation!

Di Bagshawe

TOOTHACHE

I have been around, and seen
                    the world!
And had my share of action.
But a visit to a dentist can,
            drive me to distraction!
I only have to see his chair,
My knees begin to quiver!
When he switches on the drill,
I really begin start to shiver!
He cannot hurt me anymore
I have finally learned to crack it,
When next he wants to see
                    my teeth,
I will send them in a packet!

Brian O'Brien

GOING DOWN THE SLUICE

A pious young Dutchman from Sluis,
Vowed he never would play fast and loose.
But admitted defeat
When a blonde down the street
Made an offer he couldn't refuse.

R Gordon

WET WEATHER ROWERS

Wet weather rowers are we
We never seem to be out when it's fine
We always wear our wet weather gear
But always arrive back soaked to the skin

Stormy clouds keep raining down
No matter where we go
Head or regatta
There the rain seemed to be.

We have heard of sunshine
And we scoff in disbelief
For no matter where we are
The rain is always there.

P J Aqltoft

UNTITLED

On my way to town on a midsummer's night
Clean shaven and looking all right

Before I meet my friends at 8 o'clock
I hit a few bars as the night begins
to rock

I get a feeling people are grinning and
staring
Maybe it's the clothes I'm wearing

I look up and down at myself to see
what is wrong
Nothing! So I move on

Time to go and meet my friends
but the grinning and staring doesn't
end

Cut yourself shaving one of them
says
So I go and look in the mirror, two
bits of tissue on my face.

M Whitehead

HOSPITAL CAPERS

I hope you enjoy your hospital stay,
But remember, once there, you *must* give way
To *blood-letting* needles,
And nurse's cold *scopes.*
Endue prodding and pummelling,
And give up *all* hope
Of ever reclaiming your privacy,
Then, worst of all: Get a visit, from *me!*

I can tell you all about my stay,
Back in 1963:
The sister was a *dragon,*
Really had it in for me!
The needles always seemed to sting,
The bedpans were ice-cold;
And *definitely* not the thing,
To use, when you wanted to *'Go!'*

When evening came, we would all flock out,
To the day room, to watch telly;
Look at *anything,* as long as we missed
The visit, from Auntie Nelly!
Then, before you knew it,
To the strains of *News at Ten,*
We all would be summoned to our beds,
Lie on plastic bricks, just like lead.

Well, I hope you enjoy your hospital stay,
And I've put your mind at rest.
I was not really being serious:
This was all said just in *jest!*
Wait! Just before you go,
I hope you have made out your will:
It's *just* a precaution, really,
In case the sister's name is *Jill!*

Martina Peters

THE CHEESE-LOVING SCOT

A Scotsman who loved eating cheese,
One day, his body did cease.
With a sporran full of Stilton,
He couldn't keep his kilt on,
And his bottom sagged down to his knees!

Neville Hawkins

LITTLE BO-PEEP

This is the story of Little Bo-Peep
Who lost her sheep whilst fast asleep.
When Bo-Peep woke she was quite alarmed -
So had a cup of tea until her nerves were calmed.

She then followed their trail through a hole in the fence
But soon realised this might not make much sense.
For an hour and a half - up hill and down dale -
Following the sheep but to no avail.

She ended up where she had started from -
Then realised that her sheep had come home!
To make sure none were lost numbers had to be checked -
But counting sheep can have a strange effect.

This is the story of Little Bo-Peep
Who lost her sheep whilst fast asleep . . .

Keith Thornley

NAUGHTY ANGEL

O I wish I were an angel,
That I had wings to fly,
The only thing that is stopping me,
Is that I would have to die.

If I was an angel,
I would do good deeds all day,
In the evening,
I would fly around and play.

If I was an angel,
I would like to eat good food,
I would have to be very careful not to burp,
Because that would be rude.

If I was an angel,
I would have to take a test,
Because if I was an angel,
They only take the best.

If I was an angel,
I would sing out loud,
If the others chased me,
I would hide behind a cloud.

I am sure if God could see me,
He would stop me and say,
If you don't behave yourself,
I'll take your wings away.

So I don't think I will be an angel,
I will wait for my time to come,
But then being an angel,
Could be rather fun . . .

M G Bradshaw

MEMORIES

I come from a family too numerous to count,
Quite daunting in fact by their large amount,
My husband who comes from a family so quiet,
Always complained that ours was a riot.

Each Sunday we would visit my mum,
Something like twenty or thirty would come,
Brothers and sisters with families in tow,
Faithfully off for the day we would go.

When my daughter was small, about five I would say,
She came home from school really puzzled one day,
Her teacher had told her without hesitation,
There's not such a word as 'appachination!'

My daughter replied, her face all aglow
'I'll ask my daddy for he's bound to know.'
her daddy in truth was somewhat bemused
Saying 'Write down a sentence in which it is used'

She looked in his eyes and said rather meek,
'But daddy, you use this word every week,
When we go to grandma's' she said with elation,
'You say that we visit the Apache nation!'

Annette Garrick

PAPER HANGING

Paper hanging's easy, or so the manuals say.
They show you how it's done in a professional way.
But I've tried it and I'll tell you if I may,
following them I managed just one piece in a day.

You must make sure all the rolls come from the same batch,
and when you cut the lengths you must ensure the patterns match.
Then when you paste the paper there is another catch.
If you get some on the table you will have a sticky patch.

You paste the paper thoroughly, you get it soaking wet,
then you must fold it neatly, there is no hurry yet.
It has to soak a little while, there's time for you to get
the next piece pasted ready, still no need to fret.

Now it's time the first piece was put up on the wall.
Starting at the top, (you will need steps if you're not tall).
Following the plumb line, with a brush you smooth it all.
Then when you reach the bottom the top begins to fall.

You dash back up the steps but tear the paper in your haste,
then find the manual has no answers when this problem's faced.
So you try to smooth the torn bit with a little bit of paste.
But it's no good so you rip it off and throw it in the waste.

You stop to calm your nerves, then back to work you go,
but the other piece was pasted half an hour ago.
Now it's stuck fast to the table, and that's another blow.
You forgot to wipe the table clean although they told you so.

For those who think it's easy I can verify it 'aint.
I'm sure that paper hanging would try the patience of a saint.
And though sometimes the smell of it can make me feel quite faint,
if I have to decorate again I'm going to stick to paint.

Ted Ingram

ON THE BALL

I'm nudging eighty, a poor old soul,
I have had to give up keeping goal.
Few keepers I am sure could boast,
Seventy years between the posts.
I've turned out each week for *Rose & Crown,*
Not once have ever let them down.
Our youngest player's full of tricks,
Then, of course, he's only sixty-six.
You guess we are a lively batch,
Fifty years since we won a match.
Age has begun to take its toll,
We have never ever scored a goal.
It is the teams we play that cause upset,
shooting dozens in our net.
The day I thought we'd have good luck,
Was the game between The *Dog & Duck.*
We'd give their lads a proper clouting,
Half team away on their pub outing.
Six players they fielded. Not a soul
to spare to mind their goal.
'Twas the hardest we had ever fought,
they only beat us *twenty - nought.*
Pub landlord, the man who keeps the score,
says the most I've let in *forty-four.*
He done his best to bring us cheer,
When we *win* a match

He'll buy the beer.

Tom E Chilton

RUBY BLUES

It's forty years since we were wed
and went to sleep in our double bed.
EE! It were grand to curl up tight
kissing and cuddling through the night.
But now luk wot's appened
to 'er I adore
she says as I kick 'er, an'
wot's more I snore!
'Will you just try to keep to yer own side at bed,
an' stop pullin' the bedclothes ower yer ed.'
Also she's frozen reight through to th' core,
an' it's me 'at kicks eiderdown off
on ta th' floor.
I just can't tek in all at she said
'Cos when I go ter sleep yer'd tek me for dead
Well now I've hed it
after 40 years wed
we've both ended up
in them blasted *twin beds*.

Doreen Atkinson

DUMB INSOLENCE

The teacher had a problem, which he'd never had before,
His pupils given half a chance would often cause uproar.
But now he found himself opposed by a boy who left him numb,
Who simply glared at all he said and remained completely dumb.

His classmates told the master that he did it every year,
He didn't like mathematics, that was the problem here.
Whoever the poor teacher was had no effect at all,
The lad just firmly shut his mouth and drove them up the wall.

The ice was broken quite by chance on a wintry afternoon,
Everyone was bored to death and the lesson finished soon.
The teacher passing down an aisle stepped on the rebel's toe,
The boy's mouth opened suddenly and out came cries of woe.

'You've squashed my foot, sir,' yelled the youth, jumping up
and down,
The teacher turned towards him, his face creased in a frown.
When he recognised the victim, his face lit up with glee,
'Well, there you are my lad, ' he said, 'at last you spoke to me.'

Peter Hicks

A BLOOMER

A very young girl, a pretty young thing
Could well have done with a piece of string
Along the street as she walked so proud.
Wolf whistles she got, and oh so loud.
Then suddenly what was in store
Elastic broke, pants near the floor
How pretty they were, all pink and lace
But around her ankles wasn't the place
What could she do, so much bare skin.
Nowhere at all for a safety pin
Without any string she looked so glum
The wind blew her skirt and showed her bum
A revelation, it was a sight
It gave us all a bit of a fright
Someone said is that the full moon
Of course it wasn't it was only just noon
If you don't want, to be seen all bare
Suggest you wear an extra pair.
Poor young girl, her face now red
Did she take the advice, that was said.

Joan Jeffries

APRON STRINGS

'I'll get you an au pair girl,' said
The wife to her spouse of ninety-three,
'She'll have to be a young one or
You'll run her off her feet.'

The old man digested the news in silence,
He was quite taken with the idea,
A young lass to make his coffee,
To take him for a beer.

The old wife looked at her old spouse sharply,
Then she smiled and tossed her head,
Realising what he had in mind,
'I'll get me an au pair man instead.'

Betty Eileen Houghland

NEW SHOES - OLD FEET

I should have known, this has happened before
Shoes can feel so comfortable when walking round the shop floor
Home is where my troubles begin
Trying to walk my new shoes in

I thought my new shoes would be a tonic
Not so! My big toe has a blister on it
Skin had rubbed off from my heel
So you can guess how I did feel

I kept putting my shoes on, taking them off
Trying to break them in, making them soft
It took time and discomfort for my sensitive skin
By then the heels and the soles of my shoes had worn thin

Me thinks, could I save myself this pain
Not wanting to go through this episode again
Next time I'll but myself a bigger pair
Cushion my feet and walk on air

Gladys C'Ailceta

CAMERA NEVER LIES

That can't be true - do let me see
oh what a sample of photography.
Look at Uncle Fred eyeing Auntie Mabel
Uncle Bill has the look of a young Clark Gable.

Cousin Sandra - bless her - asleep in her Silver Cross Pram
do you remember how we used to dip her soother in jam
and Uncle Tom arm-in-arm with Aunt Marie - what a honey
her blonde hair plaited around her ears - doesn't it look funny.

There stands Grandpa - always booted and suited
complete with gold watch and chain - a corker undisputed.
Oh - Kath did we really wear liberty bodices over our vests
I can see yours peeping through your Sunday best dress.

What about my brothers - camera shy Harry and John
in identical Aertex shirts - their shorts look a bit long.
And here is Mum protecting someone so shy
who wouldn't have said boo to a goose (I've learnt a lot since)
yes that was I.

Lucy Green

THE DRAGON

St George wasn't tall in fact he was a midget
Himself
He was so small he was regarded as an elf
So hearing stories of this creature down at
The pond
Made his way to the water, past the woods beyond
Reaching his destination, saw this horrid creature
Sitting on a log
Taking out a large darning needle, he killed
The dragon. A large bull frog.

Raymond J Bullock

MIRROR ON THE WALL

Mirror, mirror on the wall . . .
I saw it all . . .
My owners, three, would look at me,
He to straighten tie, pull back
His slouching shoulders, she
To pout lipstick and pat her hair,
And sonny boy, with less respect
Put out his tongue and make a face . . .
I knew my place
To keep their secrets well.

Good thing I did, you know I saw
Him intercept pink letters early . . .
Until she found one, you should hear
Her tears and rage, she tore
Out of the house and went to mother
Taking sonny boy . . .
                    I saw
The pert face of another
A younger model, and she spent
More time than ever
Pouting, settling her hair . . .
Oh I was there
When they had that bust-up, you
Should have heard the words that flew,
Slam of front door! But I knew
To keep their secrets too.

Alone and peeling after years
And cobwebs in the hall . . .
The breakers came one day and one
Without a word swung his pick
And shattered me . . . A breaker's boy
Picked up a shard of me to comb
His dreadful greasy hair . . . let fall
The last of me with all my secrets . . .
I saw it all . . .

Austin Cooper

THE FIGHT OF THE CENTURY

The White Knight and the Black Knight
Were enemies of old.
The blood was bad between them
And both were very bold
They met one evening at the Ball
The gauntlet was thrown down.
And White Knight versus Black Knight
Was the hottest fight in town.
They held it in the castle keep
Though both were out of breath.
They said they'd settle it for good
And battle to the death.
The fight raged back and forth for hours
Till White Knight had some luck
With one fell stroke the Black Knight's head,
Was rolling in the muck.
The White Knight had it mounted
On the spikes above the gate.
Then suddenly a serf appeared
And yelled 'Am I too late?
How is the Black Knight doing?
I've backed him to the hilt,
I really hope sincerely
His blood has not been spilt.'
The keeper of the gate walked up
Despite his creaking joints,
'There's your Black Knight sir' he said,
'He's *just a head on points!*'

Norman Chandler

THREE P'S FOR PETER

They'd been out for the day
And their tired son lay
Asleep, in the back of the *Humber;*
They carried him in
About to begin
To rouse the wee soul from his slumber.

When his weary dad said
'Let's just put him to bed
And not bother with toilet or food;'
'But he's hungry,' said mum,
'And a pain in his tum
Will certainly do him no good.'

'He also must be
Fair desperate to pee
After all the long journey we've done;
It just wouldn't be right
To leave him all night;
You really should think of your son!'

They argued the toss -
But she is the boss,
So dad knew what he had to do;
He wakened the lad,
And then Peter had
A pee and a pie and a poo!

Jean Scott

HIDE AND SEEK

I close my eyes, hands cover my face
I hear you running, to hide is a race
I'm near a hundred, with anticipation I'm hot
I uncover my eyes, shout, 'Coming ready or not'
First I look around, to try to catch a sight
I peer over the walls, look left and look right
I'm running around, but it's always in vain
Whenever we play it's always the same
You're always quicker and better than me
So today, I've left you hiding, I've gone for my tea!

L Higgins

AIRMAIL

Sitting comfortably? Then I'll begin my short tale,
It should make you chuckle, and maybe even wail,
It was a bright and sunny day when I drove off up the road,
To the small corner shop, that is at odd times closed,
I had some letters to post, there were quite a few,
But first they needed stamps, so I went and joined the queue,
I bought all that I needed and handed over my money,
But the events that followed I just didn't find that funny,
With the letters I stepped outside, the loose stamps in-between,
The pantomime was about to start, I didn't want to be seen,
I tried to stick the stamps on, but they started to blow away,
Like confetti in the wind they fluttered, this really wasn't my day,
Frantically I chased around, they had scattered everywhere,
I was getting seriously rattled, and my mouth began to swear,
Into gardens and onto flowers, they teased and taunted me,
They wouldn't let me catch them, and wanted to stay free,
I grabbed wildly as the stamps swirled beside my feet,
But in the end I just gave up, and had to admit defeat,
I had retrieved a couple of stamps, but they weren't really enough,
To post all the letters I had, and I stood there out of puff,
I worked out how many stamps I needed, and went and bought
some more,
On leaving the shop I went straight to my car, and quickly shut
the door,
There in safety, away from the breeze, I laid the letters on a seat,
I licked and stuck the stamps on, my mission was almost complete,
At last I posted the letters, and the lesson I've learnt is don't try,
To stick all your stamps on outside or they'll end up in the sky!

Stephen Norris

A MEDICAL BREAKTHROUGH?

A link between PMT/BSE
has always been my belief . . .
one's got something to do with mad cows -
and the other's to do with beef . . .

Sue Millward

DANNY DRUFF

When Danny Druff is on the scene
He looks like flakes of snow
And though you try to wash him out
He will not budge or go
And when you think you're rid of him
If that is not enough
He's like a flipping boomerang
That evil Danny Druff!

Linda French

GRAN

They leer at you through the glass,
Gran's teeth - built to last.
She has little hair left to comb
And she lives in a nursing home.

To gin she is very partial.
She knocks it back by the glassful.
A stick she uses, for the wrong purpose!
She brandishes it while she curses.

Her memory is a trifle weak.
She remembers last year, not last week.
She loses her glasses and has a doze
And then finds them on the end of her nose.

Helen Cronin

THE CIRCUS

The Circus is coming today,
That's what I heard people say,
There are camels with humps,
Leopard that jumps,
I hope it will be OK.

The circus is coming today,
'Hip, hip, hooray,'
There are llamas that spit,
Bears that sit,
And of course the people who pay.

There's elephants to ride,
And monkeys who hide,
And midgets to make you laugh.
Lions roar,
Trapezes sour,
And clowns that take a bath.

I'll never forget that day,
When the circus came our way,
The children cheered,
Someone jeered,
Then it all went away.

Pamela Cooper

LIMERICK

A young man from Tipton-on-Sea
sought to stretch his vocabulary;
he swallowed a dictionary, covers and all
but the extra knowledge led to his fall,
and he died of felo-de-se.

Geraldine Squires

THE INANIMATE FRIEND

Just how selfish can you get, you leave me alone and in the dark.
And then expect me to respond immediately, with the ever
  ready spark.
You sit there looking smug, as you drive past friends with a
  superior haughty smile.
And then expect me to behave with utmost consideration as you cover
  mile after mile.
Well, one of these days, I'm going to take the smile off your face,
  I'll show you who is master.
I'll wait until we're in a remote spot and refuse to budge, to you
  it will be disaster.
Looking under the bonnet, none of it makes any sense.
You panic, the confidence that you like to show, is really all
  pretence.
So once more, when you're motoring, perhaps you'll have a little
  more respect.
For, like 'Herbie', this slave of yours could have a mind of
  its own that you never did suspect.

Reg Morris

MITIGATING CIRCUMSTANCES

'Now,' said the judge, 'How do you plead?
Are you guilty of this dreadful deed?'
The prisoner said, 'Oh, hear my tale.
When first I landed in the gaol,
It was a trifling matter then.
A bit of copying with my pen.
Another prisoner shared my cell.
And life became a living hell.
His stories full of gloom and doom
Went round and round our little room.
The illnesses of his relations
The one theme of his conversations.
The sole enjoyment of his life
Was tales of woe and mournful strife.
As time went on my nerves got weaker,
Listening to this fearful speaker.
Until one day, to end it all
I bashed his head against the wall.
'Stop, stop!' He cried, 'oh, spare me, do,'
'No,' I replied, 'I'll murder you,
So you can stop your protestations -
And go and join your late relations!'

Margaret M Osoba

WORMS

How do worms,
Come to terms,
Deep down in their black pit.
They follow the arrows,
But then the road narrows,
It is always poorly lit.
Going sideways is easy,
The ups and downs are queasy,
That is the difficult bit.

Joyce Turner

THE KNIGHT IN DISTRESS

It was a dark and stormy night,
Followed by a bright and sunny day;
To a fair damsel said a brave knight,
'Let's go a-roaming far away!'

They went and walked for miles and miles;
He's got a game knee, she a huge blister . . .
A grim expression replaced her smiles,
Even before he tried to kiss 'er . . .

As they returned exhausted that night
Such dark and stormy was her mood
That our brave and handsome knight
Went roaming a-new, as far as he could . . .

He cursed his knee and her huge blister
And vowed - quite rashly - in his despair,
Never again to try and kiss 'er,
To steer clear - in future - of the damsel fair!

Daniela M Davey

SPICY FASHION FAD

The Spice Girls are leading the field
With their platform shoes they are well-heeled,
They make them look tall
'Till they head for a fall
And the bones of their ankles might yield!

Mande Newton

CULINARY DELIGHT

You are my little masterchief
My angel of delight.
When I think of your sausage roll
I apple turnover all night.

You like my suet dumpling
And my toad in the hole.
I like your pickled walnuts
And salami most of all.

C Sortino

UNTITLED

There was a young lady named Dee
Who got stung on the bum by a bee,
To add to her pain,
She went out in the rain,
And got stung once again on the knee.

P H Blackford

INFORMATION

We hope you have enjoyed reading this book - and that you will continue to enjoy it in the coming years.

If you like reading and writing poetry drop us a line, or give us a call, and we'll send you a free information pack.

Write to :-
Arrival Press Information
1-2 Wainman Road
Woodston
Peterborough
PE2 7BU
(01733) 230762